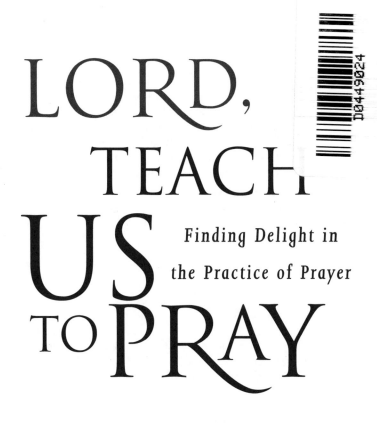

LORD, TEACH US TO PRAY

Finding Delight in
the Practice of Prayer

By Fred A. Hartley III

NAVPRESS

NAVPRESS🟊

NavPress is the publishing ministry of The Navigators, an international Christian organization and leader in personal spiritual development. NavPress is committed to helping people grow spiritually and enjoy lives of meaning and hope through personal and group resources that are biblically rooted, culturally relevant, and highly practical.

For a free catalog go to www.NavPress.com
or call 1.800.366.7788 in the United States or 1.800.839.4769 in Canada.

Dedication

*To my Lilburn Alliance Church family as we become
a house of prayer for all nations.*

Contents

Introduction

"LORD, TEACH US TO PRAY." THEY SOUND LIKE INNOCUOUS, ALMOST harmless little words. Only five of them. But don't be fooled. This might be the most dangerous little prayer you ever say to God. It has the potential to radically transform your life. Once you learn to pray, there is nothing that God wants you to have that you can't receive from Him.

"Lord, teach us to pray" is an essential prayer because we all share a common problem: none of us knows how to pray. Sure we can say the words. We can sound pious. But when it comes to mountain-quaking, heaven-moving, hell-shaking, life-transforming prayer—probably not. There's no such thing as a natural born pray-er. We don't have what it takes. When it comes to prayer, we all need help.

Prayer has caused more people to feel like miserable failures than any other Christian discipline. Even the Bible talks about our propensity to falter at prayer: "There is . . . no one who seeks God" (Ro. 3:11), and "We do not know what we ought to pray" (Ro. 8:26).

What about you? Have you ever felt like a failure at prayer? Perhaps you have made one or more of these statements:

"My prayers sound so childish."
"There I am, all alone, talking to the lamp shade."
"I am successful at other things, but when it comes to prayer I feel like a bumbling idiot."
"I try hard, but I always feel like I have a low-octane prayer life."
"Praying makes me feel awkward."
"Some people seem to get answers to prayer, but not me!"

If you can identify with any of these, there is good news. You qualify for this study! In fact, the words "Lord, teach us to pray" were first spoken by a group of people who were struggling with the same issues. The early disciples knew they needed help and they knew where to go to get it. They went right to Jesus, the Master Pray-er, and boldly asked Him!

For the next 12 weeks, you will be doing just that: Sitting at the feet of the Master, learning how to enjoy a meaningful, authentic prayer life. The lessons are taken right from the gospels, the records of the life of the Lord Jesus Christ Himself. Just as Jesus taught His disciples to pray, so He will teach you.

You can complete the lessons on your own or with a group of other seekers. Either way, you will not be alone. Christ will be with you each step of the way. Anticipate a season of accelerated spiritual growth as God answers the request, "Lord, teach us to pray."

A final word of encouragement: The fact that you would pick up a book on prayer probably indicates that God is already at work in you. There is a good chance that He has already put within you the motivation to learn to pray. Get ready for what may be the most exciting, action-packed journey of your life!

> "The sin of prayerlessness is one of the deepest roots of all evil. In it are embedded all the other sins of pride, arrogance, independence, self-sufficiency, unbelief and rebellion. And it is the one sin to which we must all plead guilty. The greatest stumbling block in the way of victory over prayerlessness is the secret feeling that we shall never obtain the blessing of being delivered from it."
> —Andrew Murray, *The Life of Prayer* (Victor House, 1981), p. 33.

Helpful Hints for the Journey

Lord, Teach Us to Pray is carefully designed to lead you into an encounter with God and mentor you to enjoy a consistent, relevant, lifelong prayer life that is more lifestyle than legalism and more delight than duty. Each lesson contains helpful assignments that will stimulate your faith and enable you to discover, firsthand from the Master, how to develop and maintain an intimate love-relationship with God.

You will have the opportunity to reflect upon, study, interact with, and memorize Bible verses that have helped Christian seekers effectively cry out to God for the past two thousand years. Questions are designed to approach each topic on four different levels (each level has a corresponding symbol, which will show up in each chapter):

✍ **Content Questions** allow you to record information from select Bible verses.

✳ **Analysis Questions** help you to analyze the information and thoughtfully interact with it.

♥ **Heart Questions** lead you to apply what you discover to your own life.

💬 **Opinion Questions** give you the chance to share your own perspective (especially stimulating in a group setting).

The five simple words, "Lord, teach us to pray," will be the "due-north" needle at all times in this study. We encourage you to do everything possible to stay on this course for maximum impact.

Lord: If you are going to learn to pray, you might as well learn from the best.

Teach: You will be learning from Jesus' formal teaching moments as well as from His example.

Us: These words were originally spoken in a group context. You may use this study as an individual; it is designed primarily, however, to be used in a group setting. God wants to teach us how to pray individually, but He also wants to teach us to pray corporately.

To Pray: We don't need yet another book about prayer; there are plenty of those. Neither do we need another book on how to pray. There

> "To pray is to let Jesus come into our hearts . . . it is Jesus who moves us to pray. He knocks. Thereby He makes known His desire to come into us. Our prayers are always the result of Jesus knocking at our hearts' doors. . . . To pray is nothing more involved than to let Jesus into our needs."
>
> — "Expounding on Revelation 3:20," O. Hallesby, *Prayer* (Augsburg Publishing House, 1959).

are plenty of how-to volumes. But we certainly need to learn to pray; to do it as a lifestyle, as a habit, as a joy and delight. That is the goal of this book. If anyone can teach us to pray, Jesus can.

Tiger Woods has his own personal golf coach. Think about it. Why would the number one golfer in the world need to hire an instructor? Because, as he pursues golfing excellence, he wants to continue to sharpen his game. The fact is, only duffers don't need coaching. Similarly, if we want to pray effectively, we need instruction. For the next 12 weeks, we will be looking to the best prayer instructor in history—Jesus Christ. He will take us out on the course and teach us how it's done properly.

Here are the main objectives:

- To encounter God and develop a deeper love-relationship with Christ.
- To study the prayer life of Jesus from the gospels.
- To learn to pray privately, particularly using the Lord's Prayer pattern.
- To learn to pray publicly or corporately in a safe environment.
- To memorize John 15:1-8 and incorporate these truths into daily life.

Blessed Lord Jesus! You live to pray, and I ask You to teach me to pray. Teach me to live to pray. In this process, cause me to share Your heavenly glory, so that I should pray without ceasing and ever stand in Your presence.

Lord Jesus! I ask You today to enroll my name among those who confess that they do not know how to pray as they ought. I especially ask You to use this course to teach me.

Lord! Teach me to persevere with You in Your "school of prayer" and offer You the time to train me. May a deep sense of my ignorance, of the wonderful privilege and power of prayer, of the need for the Holy Spirit in prayer lead me to cast away what I think I know and make me kneel before You in true teachableness and poverty of spirit.

Fill me, Lord Jesus, with a deep confidence that, because You are the Great Teacher, I will indeed learn to pray. In the assurance that my Teacher is the Lord Jesus Himself, who is ever praying to the Father on my behalf and by His prayer rules the destinies of the church and the world, I will not be afraid. I believe that You will unfold for me as much as I need to know of the mysteries of the prayer world. And where I may not know, please teach me to be strong in faith, giving glory to You.

Blessed Lord! I ask You not to put to shame this humble scholar who trusts in You, nor by Your grace will I be put to shame either. Amen.

—Andrew Murray, *With Christ in the School of Prayer*, (paraphrased).

Guidelines for Individual Study

This is not designed to be a fasten-your-seatbelts, high-speed crash course in prayer. On the contrary, we have tried to remove the risks so that you can relax, be yourself, and enjoy your Lord. Prayer should not intimidate you any longer. As prayer becomes a lifestyle, you will see that you can take God seriously without taking yourself too seriously.

Guideline #1: As you approach God, be yourself. He knows your zip code. He reads your mind. He knows what's in your closet. He smells your breath and he knows what you had for lunch. He not only knows your fingerprint, He gave it to you. So put away the flowery religious clichés. Stay away from smoke and mirrors. As you will see over and over during the next 12 weeks, Jesus relates well to all manner of people with one exception: He doesn't tolerate phonies, fakers, and pretenders. As you approach Him, remember that God loves you just for showing up.

Guideline #2: As you approach God, bring your Bible. It is the "official" prayer book. It enables you to talk with God in His "native language." Particularly when you don't know what to say, the Bible helps fill in the blanks. Saying "Lord, teach us to pray" is an example of talking to God in His own language (Lk. 11:1). In addition, you will learn to use the prayer pattern that Jesus gave His disciples in response to that request, traditionally known as the Lord's Prayer.

Guideline #3: As you approach God, give Him the freedom to change, even revolutionize, you. It will happen from the inside out. When He does it, it will be permanent. You may have even learned some bad prayer habits over the years. Like a bad golf swing, you may need to let those habits go as you replace them with better ones. All prayers are not created equally. Some are selfish, twisted, even counterproductive. Allow God to take apart, reshape, and repattern your prayer life according to God's Word.

Guideline #4: As you approach God, remember the refreshing principle that "brief is beautiful." God puts no premium on long-winded prayers. Virtuosos do not impress God. They are as boring to Him as they are to us. Cut to the chase. You don't need to beat around the bush, bow and curtsy five times, or sound eloquent to get His attention. Neither do you need to speak more softly or change your voice when you address God. He *likes* the sound of your everyday voice. After all, He gave it to you.

Guideline #5: As you approach God, enjoy Him. Have a good time! You can be sure God will enjoy the time you spend with Him. He created you for fellowship and has been patiently waiting for you to pursue intimacy with Him. One of the goals of the next several weeks is to change your prayer life from duty to delight. Allow your love for God to become what motivates every area of your life—starting with your prayer life.

Guidelines for Group Study

Each lesson has been prepared for a 90-minute class. You can adjust the lessons to as little as 60 minutes or as much as two hours. If your group is "co-ed," there may be times when you want to separate the men and women to facilitate greater freedom for sharing.

It is essential that each class include the three equally important components of 1) instruction and discussion of content; 2) interaction and application; and 3) intercession and group prayer.

Use the guidelines below to help you plan each session:

Guideline #1: Everyone approaches the group as a learner and an equal. The group leader is really more a facilitator and fellow learner than an expert who has all the answers.

Guideline #2: All questions are good questions. The group should cultivate respect for all group members so they feel it's a safe place to freely express themselves.

Guideline #3: All members participate. Try to solicit comments from every person. Do not allow anyone to dominate or anyone to hide.

Guideline #4: Stay on track. This course has been carefully written to avoid tangents or bunny trails.

Guideline #5: Spend time praying together. Some members may feel awkward praying out loud, but the only way to learn to pray is to do it. While no one should feel pressured to pray out loud, everyone should be given the opportunity. Prayer exercises are provided for each lesson.

Guidelines for the Teacher-Facilitator

We encourage you to spend 30 to 60 minutes each week, in addition to doing the lesson, studying the material. Think and pray about which questions should be emphasized. You will not have time to read through every question and discuss every answer during class time. You will need to choose an emphasis ahead of time. Pray for each of your students each week. Call a few of them each week to solicit feedback on the class or to allow them to voice any concerns. Ask the Holy Spirit to fill and control your life and to be at work during class time. Be blessed and be a blessing!

Observing the Master Pray-er

Learning from the Master

Luke 11:1-13

MAKE NO MISTAKE ABOUT IT! THE PRAYER LIFE OF JESUS WAS SO dynamic, so compelling, so radical, so infectious that the people who were closest to Him begged, "Lord, teach us to pray." They had seen all kinds of prayer, but they had never seen anything like this before. His prayer life was so categorically superior to their own that they did not want to miss the opportunity to enlist themselves in Prayer 101 with Jesus as the instructor.

Living 600 generations later has removed us from the up-close-and-personal dynamic of being taught by Jesus. It would be easy to argue, "Well sure, if I had been traveling with Jesus for three years in Palestine, I would have felt comfortable asking Him to make me a praying person too. But this is different. He doesn't live in this high-tech computer age. It's not so simple anymore." Wrong. We are at no disadvantage.

Jesus is still teaching His followers to pray. He hasn't lost His touch.

Read Luke 11:1.
The words "Lord, teach us to pray" have been called the most important prayer we will ever utter, because when you learn to pray, you can receive everything God wants you to have. This verse records the historic moment when these five words were first spoken.

✍ 1. What prompted Jesus' followers to ask, "Lord, teach us to pray"?

❋ 2. Specifically, what might they have observed?

✍ 3. What do we learn here about John the Baptizer?

♥ 4. How would you have felt if you were there with these first century followers of Christ?

🗨 5. Why do you think the words "Lord, teach us to pray" are referred to as "the most important prayer we will ever pray"?

Read Luke 11:2-10.

❋ 6. Was Jesus ready and eager to give an answer, or tentative and reluctant to respond to their request? What does this tell us about Jesus?

❋ 7. In future lessons, we will look more closely at the Lord's Prayer as a pattern (vs. 2-4). But at first glance, what strikes you about this prayer?

✍ 8. Following the Lord's Prayer, Jesus tells an interesting story about a guest at midnight (vs. 5-10). What is the point or prayer principle of this story?

9. What contemporary story could you use or create to illustrate the same principle? Write just a few details below.

10. What is the difference between asking, seeking, and knocking? Why are the three strung together in this succession?

11. Of these three forms of prayer—asking, seeking, knocking—which do you think is the most common? Least common? Why?

> "God likes to see His people shut up to this, that there is no hope but in prayer. Herein lies the Church's power against the world."
>
> —Andrew Bonair, 1853, *Heavenly Springs* (Banner of Truth Trust, 1904), p. 15.

Read Luke 11:11-13.

12. Which common, everyday household items does Jesus refer to?

13. In what way is our relationship to God the Father similar to the parent-child relationship? Not similar?

14. Is this word picture of a parent-child love relationship one with which you can identify? Why or why not?

✤ 15. What is the significance of asking for the Holy Spirit? Is there a connection between the original request (Lord, teach us to pray) and the Lord's final answer (ask for the Holy Spirit)?

♥ 16. On a scale of 1 to 10 (10 being high), how would you rank your current private prayer life? Your corporate prayer life?

♥ 17. Specifically, what would you like to see Jesus do for you during this course?

♥ 18. Is there anything that might keep Him from fulfilling this request?

♥ 19. What truth is God teaching you in this lesson? Write it down.

♥ 20. What are you going to do with this truth?

Assignment for This Week (for personal or group study)
- Each day, pray "Lord, teach us to pray."
- Read John 15:1-8.
- Sign the "Lord, Teach us to Pray" Commitment below.
- Read Luke chapters 1-12, marking "P" in the margin every time you find people praying or talking about prayer and "HS" every time you read about the Holy Spirit.
- Swap names, phone numbers, and e-mail addresses with your group members and record them in the back of your study guide.

Group Prayer Activity

- Call on someone to pray as you begin class. (Ask the person ahead of time to make sure it's okay.)
- Encourage everyone to say in unison, "Lord, teach us to pray."

"Lord, Teach Us to Pray" Commitment

- I desire a consistent, genuine prayer life and I will ask, "Lord, teach us to pray."
- I purpose to complete every lesson.
- I will attempt to use the Lord's Prayer pattern each of these 12 weeks.
- I will memorize John 15:1-8.
- I will consider recruiting a prayer partner with whom I can consistently share needs and regularly pray.

Name: _____ Date: _____

Looking to the Master

The Gospel of Luke

> "Superficiality is the curse of our age. The doctrine of instant satisfaction is a primary spiritual problem. The desperate need today is not for a greater number of intelligent people, or gifted people, but for deep people."
>
> —Richard Foster, *Celebration of Discipline*, (HarperSan Francisco), p. 1.

IT IS NO ACCIDENT THAT WHEN JESUS ASCENDED INTO HEAVEN, ALL HE left behind was a prayer meeting. That prayer meeting was His strategic masterpiece. It would become the centerpiece of history.

From the moment Jesus called His disciples to leave their fishing nets and tax offices, He had a specific goal in mind: to build the upper room prayer meeting in Jerusalem. It would be into that upper room prayer meeting that He would pour out His Holy Spirit. And it would be outward from that prayer meeting that He would send His empowered people to reach a needy world.

Jesus enrolled His followers in His "school of prayer." For three years, He strategically built prayer into every area of their lives. He knew that if He could teach them to pray, He would never need to worry about them. He could do anything through them.

Prayer was as central to Jesus' ministry as a skeletal system is to a body. If prayer somehow could have been removed from His ministry, it would have had no substance and collapsed like a pile of skin with no bones.

From the gospel of Luke, pay special attention to the mention of moments when Jesus was caught in the act of praying or was found teaching His followers to pray.

Read Luke 3:21.

✍ 1. What was Jesus doing while He was being baptized?

Read Luke 4:1-14.

✳ 2. Before Jesus began His public ministry, why was it so important for Him to spend 40 days praying and fasting?

Read Luke 5:16 and Luke 9:28.

✍ 3. What do you learn about Jesus in these verses?

Read Luke 6:12.

✳ 4. Why was it important for Jesus to spend the entire night praying prior to calling His 12 disciples? What might some of His prayers have sounded like?

Read Luke 9:18-20.

✳ 5. Before Jesus asked the significant question "Who do you say I am?", why was it important that He pray for His followers?

Read Luke 9:28-36.

❇ 6. What was Jesus doing while He was praying? What is the significance?

Read Luke 19:45-46.

This passage reports one of the most intensely passionate and emotional moments in Jesus' life. It almost seems out of character for Jesus to appear so angry.

✍ 7. What did Jesus intend to communicate when He said, "My house will be a house of prayer"? Why was He so passionate about it?

Read Luke 22:39-46.

❇ 8. What do we learn about Jesus by the fact that He spent His final night with the disciples in prayer?

Read Luke 24:49.

✍ 9. What was Jesus' final command to His followers, according to Luke's gospel?

Read Acts 1:4,14.

✍ 10. What was the only thing Jesus left here on earth when He ascended into heaven?

🗭 11. Put a "J" in front of the words that accurately describe Jesus' prayer life. Put an "M" in front of the words that accurately describe your own prayer life.

___ Dynamic	___ Joyful	___ Intentional	___ Life-giving
___ Boring	___ Monotonous	___ Strategic	___ Relevant
___ Effective	___ Habitual	___ Mystical	___ Catalytic
___ Vital	___ Consistent	___ Miraculous	___ (Other)

🗭 12. What did you find surprising or even shocking about Jesus' prayer life?

♥ 13. What truth is God teaching you in this lesson? Write it down.

♥ 14. What are you going to do with that truth?

Assignment for This Week (for personal or group study)
- Continue to pray daily, "Lord, teach us to pray."
- Read Luke 13-24, marking "P" in the margin every time you find people praying or talking about prayer and "HS" every time you read about the Holy Spirit.
- Memorize John 15:1.

Group Prayer Activity
- Share what you have learned through your reading of Luke 1-12.
- As you begin the class, encourage each person to complete the sentence, "Lord, I thank You for . . ."

Our Master's Prayer Pattern

Matthew 6:9-13

> "We do not want to be beginners. But let us be convinced of the fact that (when it comes to prayer) we will never be anything else but beginners all our life!"
>
> —Thomas Merton, *Contemplative Prayer*
> (Doubleday and Company., Inc., 1969), p. 37.

ONLY 52 WORDS. YOU CAN SAY IT IN LESS THAN 20 SECONDS WITHOUT even taking a breath. Yet the Lord's Prayer covers all the things we'd ever want to express to God.

It is the only prayer pattern God has given us. It is not simply a pattern, however; it is God's own Word. He has given it for us to use freely with Him every day.

No group of words has ever been strung together with more potential than these. Yet despite all this, over the centuries believers haven't had a clue how to put it to good use.

For generations, the prayer has been inaccurately referred to as the Lord's Prayer. In reality, however, our Lord would not have used this prayer as His own because it says "forgive us our sins" — and He never sinned. For this reason, in this study we will refer to it as the Lord's Prayer pattern, or the pattern Jesus gave His followers.

Over the next six lessons, you will be learning what each phrase of this prayer was intended to mean. You will also learn how to incorporate it into your daily time with God to maximize your effectiveness in prayer.

There are six distinct portions to the Lord's Prayer pattern:

1. Relationship: *"Our Father in heaven"*

God intends us to begin each day by reminding ourselves of His loving relationship with us. Many people think the Lord's Prayer pattern starts with worship, but it doesn't. It starts with relationship. Without a relationship, there is no starting point for prayer (except in the case of a salvation prayer). All real prayer flows out of God's radical love for us. So it is good to remind ourselves that we pray *from* a relationship, not *toward* a relationship. For this reason, Jesus begins our prayer pattern by acknowledging that relationship.

2. Worship: *"Hallowed be your name"*

The prayer then moves to worship. How can we spend time with a God who loves us so completely without breaking into worship? The heart of worship flows out of an accurate view of God's identity—His name. As we grow in prayer, we grow into a better understanding of God's character, His nature, His attributes. He teaches us how to pray His name effectively and strategically over our own lives and the lives of others. This hallowing of God's name is high on His priority list, so it is high on our prayer list.

3. Lordship: *"Your kingdom come, your will be done"*

The three "your" statements—"your name . . . your kingdom . . . your will"—firmly rivet our prayer into God's agenda, not ours. These three statements are sequential, moving from God's person ("your name") to God's purposes ("your kingdom") to God's plans ("your will"). The "your" statements form a safeguard for our prayer pattern, keeping us God-centered, kingdom-minded, and obedient.

4. Sonship: *"Give us . . . Forgive us"*

The two most basic needs of children are food and forgiveness. For this reason, Jesus wants us to approach our Father on a daily basis to receive both. It is significant that the request for food comes first. If you or I had written this prayer, we probably would have put the confession of personal sin up front—as if God would not answer the other portions of the prayer until we had confessed our sin. God is clearly more forgiving than we are. After all, it is God's kindness that leads us to repentance.

5. Fellowship: *"As we also have forgiven"*

Having received forgiveness for our sins from the Father, we are now able to extend forgiveness to others for their sins against us. Forgiveness is an essential element in maintaining healthy interpersonal relationships. And healthy interpersonal relationships are an essential element of prayer. This part of the pattern helps us to pull the weeds of bitterness and resentment from the garden of our hearts every day—before they have the opportunity to grow into life-destroying bushes or trees.

6. Leadership: *"Lead us . . . deliver us"*

Once we have processed through all these portions of the Lord's Prayer pattern, we are ready to ask for God's leadership and deliverance. This is actually the high point of the prayer—to firmly align our will with God's will.

Perhaps you have wondered, "Why do I need to ask God not to lead me into temptation? A holy God wouldn't do that!" It is true that it's impossible for God, who is exclusively good, to tempt us with evil. Yet we know from God's Word that He loves us to earnestly seek Him for what He already wants for us. He wants us to vehemently hate evil and seek His delivering power in the same way He wants us to diligently pursue good. Therefore, it is important to pray for power to withstand the evil one and his schemes.

The Lord's Prayer pattern is the "meat and potatoes" of this study. We will interact with it, become well acquainted with it, and make it like a best friend.

Read Matthew 6:9-13.

✍ 1. Did Jesus say, "This is what to pray" or "This is how you should pray"? What is the difference?

✻ 2. What do the words "Our Father in heaven" tell us about God? What do they tell us about our relationship with God?

✻ 3. Why is it important to start all prayer with the reminder that we have a love relationship with God?

✻ 4. In what way is the honoring of God's name central to worship and essential to prayer?

✍ 5. What are the three "your" statements? What effect are they intended to have on the pray-er?

✻ 6. What does the term "lordship" mean? How does this apply to your daily lifestyle? To your prayer life?

💬 7. What is the difference between God-centered praying and man-centered praying?

✻ 8. What does the phrase "give us today our daily bread" tell us about ourselves?

✻ 9. What does the phrase "give us today our daily bread" tell us about God?

💬 10. Why is it important for us to receive forgiveness daily?

💬 11. Why is it important for us to extend forgiveness daily?

✱ 12. In what way do our interpersonal relationships affect our relationship with God?

✱ 13. Why is it important for us to pray "lead us not into temptation"?

⌐ 14. Why did Jesus save "but deliver us from the evil one" until the end of the prayer pattern?

♥ 15. What truth is God teaching you in this lesson? Write it down.

♥ 16. What are you going to do with this truth?

Assignment for This Week (for personal or group study)
- Review the gospel of Luke and note where you marked a "P" for prayer and "HS" for Holy Spirit. Do you see a pattern? What insights did you learn from this exercise?
- Quote John 15:1 to a friend from memory.
- Memorize John 15:2-3.
- One day this week, take five minutes or more to begin praying the Lord's Prayer pattern.

Group Prayer Activity
- Ask everyone in class to share a name of God he or she has come to know through experience. Ask each person to share the story.
- Spend up to 10 minutes in open, spontaneous group prayer, declaring the names of God and worshiping Him for who He is.

Experiencing Our Master's Prayer Pattern

Seeking His Heart

Relationship: John 15:1-8

"Our Father in heaven"

> "The essence of idolatry is the entertainment of thoughts about God that are unworthy of Him."
>
> —A. W. Tozer, *The Knowledge of the Holy*
> (Harper and Row, 1961), p. 11.

RELATIONSHIP IS THE ESSENCE OF PRAYER. FOR THIS REASON, THE PRAYER pattern Jesus gave us begins with the relational phrase, "Our Father in heaven." As believers, we do not simply pray toward a relationship with God; we pray *from* a relationship with God. We already have an intimate relationship with Him and He wants us to enjoy it.

One of the great dangers to prayer is a purely utilitarian view of it; that is, thinking that the primary reason to pray is to *get* something from God. The primary reason to pray, rather, is to *be* with God. At times we will receive tangible gifts or answers to prayer, and at times we will receive something even more valuable: a revelation of who He is and who we are in relationship with Him.

The reason Jesus began the Lord's Prayer pattern with the words "Our Father in heaven" was to tune us in to His love for us as we begin to pray. God wants us to realize that He doesn't only love us when we pray. He loves us just as much when we don't pray. There is nothing we can ever do to make Him love us any more—and there is nothing we can ever do to make Him love us any less! The problem is that we often fail to *experience* His love when we neglect our prayer life. So Jesus encouraged us to begin our prayers each day with "Our Father in heaven."

Many, many people have such shallow encounters with God that they never develop a healthy, intimate relationship with Him. Knowing that He would soon be leaving His disciples behind, Jesus addressed this issue. He didn't want His disciples wandering off, distancing themselves, or simply becoming nostalgic. He didn't want them—or us—to have shallow encounters with God. He jealously longs for a life-changing, ever-deepening relationship with us—it's the reason He went to the cross.

Read John 15:1-8.

Jesus used the word picture of the intimate, life-sustaining relationship between the branch and the vine to describe the relationship between Him and His followers. You will be memorizing this word picture over the next several weeks to help you gain familiarity with these vital verses.

Note the key words in John 15:1-8:

Remain: Used 11 times, this word refers to our love relationship with Jesus.

Fruit: Used nine times, this word refers to the relevance of the love relationship with Jesus.

❋ 1. List several ways in which God resembles a gardener (v. 1).

❋ 2. List several ways in which Jesus resembles a vine (vs. 1-3).

❋ 3. List several ways in which we as Christ's followers resemble branches (vs. 3-7).

✣ 4. In what way does the word *remain* accurately depict our love relationship with Christ?

✣ 5. We know what it means for a branch to remain on the vine. What does it mean for us to "remain" in Christ?

✏ 6. What is pruning (v. 2)? What is the purpose of pruning? How does it take place?

♥ 7. Have you ever experienced pruning in your life? Explain the situation.

✣ 8. According to verses 7 and 8, what is "fruit"?

✣ 9. According to verse 7, what is necessary for us to receive miraculous answers to our prayers?

🗩 10. In what way do answers to prayer bring glory to God?

♥ 11. If your life were to be represented by a vine, how healthy and fruitful would it appear?

✹ 12. According to verses 1-8, what role does the Word of God play in our relationship with God in general and in our prayer life specifically?

✹ 13. What does John 15 have to do with the words "Our Father in heaven?"

♥ 14. Complete this sentence: "In this study so far, what God has taught me about my relationship with Him is _____ —."

✹ 15. What truth is God teaching you in this lesson? Write it down.

♥ 16. What are you going to do with this truth?

Assignment for This Week (for personal or group study)
• One day this week, use the six parts of the Lord's Prayer pattern in your prayer time.
• Quote John 15:1-3 to a friend from memory.
• Begin memorizing John 15:4-5.
• Consider recruiting a prayer partner. If you are using this study guide in a group, consider selecting a prayer partner from the group.
• Write down the six parts of the Lord's Prayer pattern from memory.

Prayer Partners

A prayer partner is someone special with whom you have agreed to pray regularly. This does not need to be a best friend, but it does need to be someone you trust. You will share (confidentially) personal prayer needs and pray for and with each other on a consistent basis. Jesus encouraged such a partnership when He said, "If two of you on earth agree about anything you ask for, it will be done for you by my Father in heaven. For where two or three come together in my name, there am I with them" (Matthew 18:19-20). There is power in agreeing in prayer with a special partner. While participating in this study, it might be a perfect time to initiate such a special partnership. Remember, a prayer partnership is:

- An agreement between two believers to pray for and with each other on a regular basis (once a month, twice a month, or weekly)
- A willingness to share personal needs
- A commitment to pray for your partner's needs
- An adventure in faith, believing God to work miracles as His Word promised

When establishing a prayer partnership, it is a good idea to decide upon a limited time frame (for example, for the next six months, or for this school year). You can always decide to extend the commitment later.

Group Prayer Activity

- Share with the group what you have been learning while using the Lord's Prayer pattern.
- Set aside 15 minutes for group prayer and pray through the first three parts of the Lord's Prayer pattern.
- Spend approximately five minutes in group prayer on the phrase "Our Father in heaven." Tell the group they can talk to God, read verses from the Bible, or sing songs related to this phrase.
- Allow another five minutes for each of the next two phrases, "hallowed be your name" and "your kingdom come, your will be done."
- Conclude by asking the group what they learned and how they felt about this activity.

Sitting at His Feet

Worship: Luke 10:38-42

"Hallowed be your name"

> "It is in the process of being worshiped that God communicates His presence to men."
>
> —C.S. Lewis

OUR FAST-PACED LIFESTYLES WORK AGAINST THE NOTION OF SITTING AT Christ's feet in worship and adoration. We tend to do everything in a hurry. We are inclined to shop in a hurry, talk in a hurry, eat in a hurry—and even pray in a hurry.

God loves to meet with you any time, whether in the car, on your exercise bike, or at the kitchen sink. But if you only talk with God while doing other activities, you'll cheat yourself out of a greater delight—and settle for a superficial relationship with Him. Surely the Creator of the universe desires more than that with you.

> "To worship is to quicken the conscience by the holiness of God, to feed the mind by the truth of God, to purge the imagination by the beauty of God, to open the heart to the love of God and to devote the will to the purposes of God."
>
> —Anglican Bishop William Temple

Read Luke 10:38-42.

Martha and Mary represent two temperamentally different people with two radically different relationships with Christ. While they grew up in the same home and were flesh and blood sisters, they bear little resemblance to one another. Neither one was a bad person, but one was commended by her Lord and the other was confronted.

✍ 1. Make a list below of words or phrases that compare and contrast these two women.

Martha   **Mary**

_____   _____

_____   _____

_____   _____

_____   _____

_____   _____

_____   _____

_____   _____

♥ 2. Which woman do you more closely resemble? In what ways?

✍ 3. What did Jesus mean when He said, "but only one thing is needed" (Luke 10:42). What is the "one thing"?

✍ 4. Again, when Jesus said, "Mary has chosen what is better, and it will not be taken away from her," to what is He referring?

�֍ 5. Both Paul and David used the expression "one thing." Paul said, "But *one thing* I do: Forgetting what is behind and straining toward what is ahead" (Philippians 3:13). David said, "*One thing* I ask of the LORD, this is what I seek: that I may dwell in the house of the LORD all the days of my life, to gaze upon the beauty of the LORD and to seek him in his temple" (Psalm 27:4). Is it fair to say the "one thing" is the same thing in these three examples? Why or why not?

✖ 6. Since Mary sat at Jesus' feet, she probably had opportunity to know and appreciate Him better than Martha. What names or attributes of Jesus might she have known by experience?

♥ 7. From the following list, which names of God can you relate to? Check all you have come to know by experience.

Names of God

__ Advocate	__ God	__ Messiah
__ Author	__ Head	__ Passover
__ Banner	__ Helper	__ Physician
__ Beloved	__ Holy Spirit	__ Prince
__ Bread of Life	__ Horn	__ Righteousness
__ Bridegroom	__ I AM	__ Rock
__ Christ	__ Immanuel	__ Ruler
__ Creator	__ Jealous	__ Savior
__ Crown	__ Jesus	__ Shepherd
__ Deliverer	__ Judge	__ Sovereign
__ Eternal Life	__ King	__ Spirit
__ Faithful	__ Lamb	__ Teacher
__ Father	__ Light	__ Voice
__ First Born	__ Lord	__ Wisdom
__ Friend	__ Maker	__ Wonderful
__ Glory	__ Master	__ Word

> "How little people know who think that holiness is dull. When one meets the real thing, it is irresistible. If even 10 percent of the world's population had it, would not the whole world be converted and happy before a year's end?"
>
> —C.S. Lewis

♥ 8. From the following list, which attributes of God have you come to know by experience? Check all you can relate to.

Attributes of God

__ All-powerful

__ All-wise

__ Anointed

__ Awesome

__ Blessed

__ Compassionate

__ Covenant-keeping

__ Creative

__ Encouraging

__ Enduring

__ Eternal

__ Everlasting

__ EverPresent

__ Exalted

__ Faithful

__ Forgiving

__ Friendly

__ Fruitful

__ Giving

__ Glorious

__ Holy

__ Hopeful

__ Indescribable

__ Invisible

__ Jealous

__ Just

__ Living

__ Long-suffering

__ Loving

__ Merciful

__ Passionate

__ Praiseworthy

__ Prayerful

__ Precious

__ Radiant

__ Redemptive

__ Relational

__ Righteous

__ Secure

__ Self-revealing

__ Sensitive

__ Serving

__ Sovereign

__ Strong

__ Truthful

__ Unchanging

__ Understanding

__ Vocal

> "Worshiping God is the great essential of fitness. If you have not been worshiping . . . when you get into work you will not only be useless yourself, but a tremendous hindrance to those who are associated with you."
>
> —Oswald Chambers, *My Utmost for His Highest*
> (Dodd, Mead and Co., 1935), p. 254.

Read Psalm 24:1-10.
This Psalm was a Hebrew song, sung on the way to temple worship. The temple stood elevated on a hill in Jerusalem, thereby giving double meaning to the phrase "who may ascend the hill of the LORD." The hill was higher in elevation as well as value or worth.

✣ 9. What does it mean for us to "ascend the hill of the LORD"?

✣ 10. Who was a better climber: Martha or Mary? Why?

♥ 11. Why do we not spend more time climbing?

♥ 12. Which of the qualifications for climbers listed in Psalm 24 have interfered with your own climbing?

♥ 13. Which of these qualifications motivates you to be more diligent in your own experience of worship?

♥ 14. What truth is God teaching you in this lesson? Write it down.

♥ 15. What are you going to do with that truth?

"The destined end of man is not happiness, nor health, but holiness. God is not an eternal blessing machine for men. He did not come to save men out of pity; He came to save men because He had created them to be holy."

—Oswald Chambers

Assignment for This Week (for individual or group study)
- Continue to use the Lord's Prayer pattern in your daily prayer life. At least one day this week, enjoy an extended time (30 or more minutes) in prayer, sitting at His feet.
- Quote John 15:1-5 from memory to a friend.
- If you have decided to recruit a prayer partner, establish a meeting time and determine ahead of time several personal prayer requests you can share with him or her.
- Look at the list of names and attributes of God on pages 41 and 42. Choose several and pray that the significant people in your life (e.g., parents, spouse, children, best friend) will experience Him in that way.

Group Prayer Activity
- At the beginning of class, encourage everyone to identify a name of God he or she has come to know by experience. Then take turns calling out these names (e.g., "Lord, I declare You as

my Provider because You have supplied me with everything I need.")

- At the end of class, enjoy another extended time of prayer, expressing to God your appreciation for His attributes. Begin each prayer with the phrase, "God, what I appreciate most about You is _____."

Lesson Six

Submitting to His Authority

Lordship: Matthew 5:1-10, 13:44-46

"Your kingdom come, your will be done"

> "Prayer must never be a substitute for obedience."
>
> —A.W. Tozer

THE THREE PHRASES, "HALLOWED BE YOUR NAME," "YOUR KINGDOM come," and "your will be done," represent a radical paradigm shift in prayer. If you really mean what you are saying when you pray these three phrases, a revolution has already begun within you.

By nature, human beings seek the fame of our *own* name, the establishment of our *own* kingdom, and the completion of our *own* will. So to pray these phrases genuinely is a 180-degree turn. It means you shift from concern over your name to God's name; from your little kingdom to His; and from your will to His.

Your name refers to God's person, His character.

Your kingdom refers to God's principles, His pattern of doing things.

Your will represents God's plan, the specific steps He wants followed.

❋ 1. Why is the sequence—"your name" (God's person), "your kingdom" (God's principles), and "your will" (God's plan)— important?

♥ 2. Have you found that any of these three phrases in the Lord's Prayer pattern disturbs you?

❊ 3. In general, which of these phrases do you consider the most overlooked or misunderstood?

Jesus taught explicitly and extensively about the kingdom of God. Most of His parables begin with "the kingdom of God is like . . ." The Sermon on the Mount (Matthew 5,6,7) contains extensive teaching about the kingdom of God. Throughout the gospels we are taught to seek the kingdom (Matthew 6:33), preach the kingdom (Matthew 24:14), live the kingdom (Mark 1:15), and pray the kingdom (Matthew 6:10).

Many pages of Christian literature have been devoted to describing the kingdom of God. This is because it's important to understand the kingdom of God in order to know how to pray it effectively. In the simplest terms, the kingdom of God is more the reign of God than a particular realm. It is more an internal force that shapes individual lives than an external force over geopolitical areas.

✐ 4. In your own words, define the kingdom of God.

✐ 5. When we pray "your kingdom come," what are we asking for?

❊ 6. Find and write down some verses from the gospels that help define what we are asking for when we pray for the coming of the kingdom.

Read Matthew 5:1-10.

These verses may be familiar to you, but it's possible that you've never viewed them as verses about the kingdom. Look more closely. Not only can they teach you about the kingdom, but they offer much you can employ in your prayer life.

✍ 7. Which of the eight "blessed are" statements specifically promise the kingdom? Why are these qualities so essential to the kingdom?

❊ 8. It has been said that each of the other "blessed are" statements also demonstrates the presence of the kingdom. In what ways is this true?

  • Those who mourn:_____

  • The meek:_____

  • Those who hunger and thirst for righteousness:_____

  • The merciful:_____

  • The pure in heart:_____

  • The peacemakers:_____

♥ 9. If each of these statements represents the kingdom, and since we are encouraged to pray the kingdom, what does it mean for us to pray these on ourselves? On our church family? On other people?

♥ 10. Which of these do you believe God desires to see more evident in your life? In your church family?

Read Matthew 13:44-46.

These verses contain two parables about the kingdom. There are many other such parables, but we will begin with these and learn ways to apply their principles to others we come across in the future.

✍ 11. What do verses 44 and 45 say the hidden treasure and the pearl are describing?

✽ 12. What do these stories show us about the kingdom?

• Hidden treasure: _____

• Pearl: _____

♥ 13. What truths from these parables can you apply to your prayer life?

♥ 14. What truth is God teaching you in this lesson? Write it down.

♥ 15. What are you going to do with this truth?

Assignment for This Week (for individual and group study)
• Continue using the Lord's Prayer pattern each day as you spend extended time with God. Keep a list of insights that God gives you.
• Several times each day, quote John 15:1-5, emphasizing each word and considering its importance.
• Begin memorizing John 15:6-7, so that next week you can quote John 15:1-7 from memory.

Group Prayer Activity
- Share with each other what you are learning while praying through the Lord's Prayer pattern on a daily basis.
- Discuss the following question: When we pray "your kingdom come," what specifically are we praying for?
- Spend some time praying on the theme "your kingdom come."

Lesson Seven

Receiving Our Inheritance

Sonship: Luke 18:9-14

"Give us . . . Forgive us"

> "Hurry is not of the Devil; it is the Devil."
>
> —C.G. Jung, Mortin T. Kelsey, *The Other Side of Silence* (Paulist Press, 1976), p. 83.

THERE ARE TWO THINGS CHILDREN NEED FROM THEIR PARENTS: FOOD and forgiveness. Jesus teaches us to come to Him to receive both daily. *"Give us today our daily bread. Forgive us our debts . . ."* These prayers reflect our daily needs as sons and daughters of God.

This portion of the Lord's Prayer pattern marks a shift in the focus of the prayer, moving from God's sufficiency (your name, your kingdom, your will) to our needs (our daily bread, our debts). It is important for us to declare our faith in God's sufficiency. It is equally important for us to declare our awareness of our dependence on Him.

❋ 1. Why does God want us to ask Him for daily bread?

🗨 2. What kind of needs are we asking for when we ask for "daily bread"?

♥ 3. How does it make you feel to ask God each day for "daily bread" kinds of needs?

✣ 4. Why does God want us to ask for forgiveness each day?

♥ 5. How does it make you feel to ask God each day for forgiveness?

"No man knows how bad he is until he has tried to be good. There is a silly idea that good people don't know what temptation means."

—C.S. Lewis

Read Luke 18:9-14.
Here is a story about two men—a study in contrast. It illustrates how religious rituals can be an enemy to a genuine spiritual life, particularly when they stimulate a phony sense of righteousness (known as self-righteousness!). There is perhaps nothing more devastating to authentic prayer than self-righteousness. Jesus clearly demonstrated that He loves the unrighteous—but cannot relate to the self-righteous.

It has been said that there are three lifestyles relating to righteousness:

- **Unrighteousness:** The lifestyle that is obviously in violation of God's law.
- **Self-righteousness:** The lifestyle that pretends to follow God's law, but is, in reality, out of step with God.
- **God's righteousness:** The lifestyle that is in step with God and His law.

✍ 6. List some of the dissimilarities between the two men in Luke 18:9-14.

Pharisee	**Tax Collector**
____________________	____________________
____________________	____________________
____________________	____________________
____________________	____________________

❇ 7. Which type of righteousness (unrighteousness, self-righteousness, or God's righteousness) characterized the Pharisee?

❇ 8. Which type of righteousness characterized the tax collector?

❇ 9. Which man left his prayer time in the temple with God's righteousness?

❇ 10. What virtue or character trait was found in the tax collector that enabled him to receive God's righteousness?

♥ 11. Which of these two men do you most relate to? Which man most closely represents the kind of prayer life you have?

12. Which of the three types of righteousness is more prevalent among nonchurch-going people?

13. Which of the three types of righteousness do you see most among church-going people?

14. What does self-righteousness look like in our world?

✱ 15. How might self-righteousness hinder a genuine work of God in someone's life?

♥ 16. What truth is God teaching you in this lesson? Write it down.

♥ 17. What are you going to do with this truth?

Assignment for This Week (for individual or group study)
- You are now more than halfway through this study. Write out a brief prayer for each of the six parts of the Lord's Prayer pattern.
- Continue to write down the insights you gain into your love relationship with God as you pray through the Lord's Prayer pattern.
- Quote John 15:1-7 from memory to a friend.
- Begin memorizing John 15:8.

Group Prayer Activity
- Share with the group general insights you are gaining from using the Lord's Prayer pattern.
- Share specific insights related to the "daily bread" portion of the prayer.
- Share insights you are learning as you memorize John 15.
- Spend time as a group praying "give us today our daily bread" for each other.

Agreeing Together

Fellowship: Mark 9:33-35, 10:35-45

"As we also have forgiven"

> "A man who confesses his sins in the presence of a brother knows that he is no longer alone with himself; he experiences the presence of God in the reality of the other person. As long as I am by myself in the confession of my sins, everything remains in the dark, but in the presence of a brother, the sin has to be brought into the light."
>
> —Dietrich Bonhoeffer, *Life Together*
> (Harper and Row, 1952), p. 116.

NOW WE COME TO AN IMPORTANT PRAYER PRINCIPLE— *YOUR RELATIONship with people affects your relationship with God.* When you are harboring ill feelings toward the people in your life, you cannot possibly be enjoying unfettered intimacy with God. This prayer principle—that our horizontal relationships with others affect our vertical relationship with God—is one we can all too easily overlook, but we will not get away with it. God loves us too much to allow us to cheat ourselves.

There were times when even the disciples did not get along well together. They faced many heated arguments due to their stubbornness, self-will, and pride.

Read Mark 9:33-35 and Mark 10:35-45.

Once in a while, it is good to realize that the early disciples were not only human; they were pridefully sinful. The Bible does not whitewash or cover over the disciples' shortcomings.

✍ 1 List below the quality traits (some of which may even be shocking) that you see in the disciples in these two passages.

Mark 9:33-35   **Mark 10:35-45**

_____   _____

_____   _____

_____   _____

♥ 2. In your interpersonal relationships, have you ever been victimized by any of these qualities? How did they make you feel?

💬 3. Why do you think these traits hinder prayer?

Read John 17:20-26.
Chapter 17 in John's gospel contains the longest of Jesus' recorded prayers. We can assume that this is a prayer that will be answered.

✍ 4. For what miracle in the lives of the disciples is Jesus praying?

❋ 5. When this miracle is realized, what effect will it have on the onlooking world?

❋ 6. What does Jesus say about why the miracle will have this effect?

♥ 7. Have you ever experienced unity with a group of other believers or other pray-ers? Describe what that was like.

🗨 8. Why is unity important to God? Why is disunity an offense?

"Everybody thinks of changing humanity and nobody thinks of changing himself."

—Leo Tolstoy, Frank S. Mead, *Ed. Religious Quotations* (Peter Davis Limited, 1965), p. 400.

Read Matthew 18:19.

The word "agree" is translated from the Greek s*umphaneo* (from which we get the word symphony). In other words, we are to pray in symphony or in concert with each other.

✍ 9. What prayer principle do you see here?

❋ 10. What does it sound like when people are praying together in symphony or in concert with one another?

❋ 11. What does it sound like when people are not praying together in symphony or in concert with one another?

12. Why do you think God places a high priority on us praying in symphony with one another?

Read Matthew 5:23-26.

Our relationship with God in prayer and worship is the highest priority. But there are times when we need to first address our relationships with each other. In these verses, Jesus teaches with conviction that we will sometimes need to temporarily lay aside worship to attend to fellowship. We need to be reconciled to each other if we are going to be reconciled to God completely. Similarly, Matthew 6:12-15 tells us that God forgives our sins to the extent that we forgive those who sin against us.

13. According to Matthew 5:23-26, when does fellowship become a more urgent priority than worship?

14. When you are facing an interpersonal conflict, what effect does it have on your prayer life?

15. Can you write down a positive example of this prayer principle?

16. What truth is God teaching you in this lesson? Write it down.

17. What are you going to do with this truth?

"By the prayers of His saints, this gives us great reason to think, that whenever the time comes that God gives an extraordinary spirit of prayer for the promised advancement of His kingdom on earth—which is God's great aim in all preceding providences, and the main thing that the spirit of prayer in the saints aims at—then the fulfillment of this event is nigh."

—Jonathan Edwards, "An Humble Attempt," *The Works of Jonathan Edwards*, vol. 2 (1834, reprinted 1976, The Banner of Truth Trust), p. 292.

Assignment for This Week (for individual or group study)
- Keep asking "Lord, teach us to pray!"
- Continue to use the Lord's Prayer pattern each day.
- Record the insights you are learning as you use the Lord's Prayer pattern.
- Quote John 15:1-8 to a friend from memory. (Congratulations! This week you finish this assignment.)
- Continue to write down your insights into your love relationship with God from John 15.

Group Prayer Activity
- Without being indiscrete or breaching another person's confidence, share with the group your answer to Question 15.
- Have you ever said to anyone, "I am sorry; I was wrong. Will you forgive me?" Without putting anyone else in a bad light, share your story with the group.
- As a group, take 20 to 30 minutes to pray through the Lord's Prayer pattern. (Approximately every five minutes, the group facilitator can move the group to the next portion by saying, "Now . . . hallowed be your name," and so on.)

Claiming His Promises

Leadership: Matthew 4:1-11

"And lead us not into temptation, but deliver us from the evil one"

THIS IS THE FINAL PORTION OF THE LORD'S PRAYER PATTERN. IN A SENSE, every preceding portion was preparation for it. The pattern is clearly sequential. If we leapfrog over one portion, we will be ill-equipped to move into the next one. For instance:

- If we are not reconciled to each other (fellowship), we will not be ready to resist the evil one (leadership).
- If we have not received forgiveness (Sonship), we will not be prepared to extend it to others (fellowship).
- If we do not have a solid bond of love with the Father (relationship), we can't come asking for food or forgiveness (Sonship).

> "Give me 100 preachers who fear nothing but sin and desire nothing but God . . . such alone will shake the gates of hell and set up the Kingdom of heaven on earth."
>
> —John Wesley, E.M. Bounds, *Power through Prayer*, p. 77.

Read Matthew 4:1-11.
When Christ faced the temptation of the evil one, He quoted Scripture—three times. This is the classic example of how to use Scripture effectively in prayer. It's a primary weapon for responding to the evil one when we, too, are tempted.

✍ 1. According to v. 1, who led Jesus out into the wilderness where He was tempted?

❋ 2. Describe the nature of the first temptation. How did Jesus respond?

♥ 3. Have you ever faced a similar temptation? Describe it. How did you respond?

❋ 4. Describe the nature of the second temptation. How did Jesus respond?

♥ 5. Have you ever faced a similar temptation? Describe it. How did you respond?

❋ 6. Describe the nature of the third temptation. How did Jesus respond?

♥ 7. Have you ever faced a similar temptation? Describe it. How did you respond?

Read 2 Peter 1:4.
The Bible is full of the promises of God—literally thousands of them! We who are familiar with warranties and insurance policies should be

able to understand the value of a promise from God. God's promises are life-giving and faith-building. They are vitally important in enabling us to follow the leadership of the Lord as well as flee the enticement of the enemy. He wants us not only to know His promises, but to put them to good use also.

✍ 8. In 2 Peter 1:4, how are the promises of God described?

✍ 9. What does the passage say are the two reasons the promises of God are given?

�֍ 10. Specifically, how can we use the promises of God to "participate in the divine nature"? Give an example.

✖ 11. Specifically, how can we use the promises of God to "escape the corruption in the world caused by evil desires"? Give an example.

♥ 12. Can you give an example of how you have used the promises of God in either way in your own life?

"The greatest miracle that God can do today is to take an unholy man out of an unholy world and make that man holy and put him back into that unholy world and keep him holy in it."

—Leonard Ravenhill

The gospel accounts of Jesus' life clearly show that our Lord loved the promises of God. If we intend to be mentored by His prayer life, we too will want to develop a love and appreciation for God's promises. We will want to learn how to use them the way our Lord did.

- Jesus *claimed* the promises of God (Matthew 4:4).
- Jesus *fulfilled* the promises of God (Luke 4:18-19).
- Jesus *gave* the promises of God

Consider some of the promises of God given to us by Jesus. Develop a good eye for spotting them as you read through the gospels. The entire Bible is full of promises, but the gospels are a good place to begin recognizing them. Here are some examples:

Binding/Loosing
"I tell you the truth, whatever you bind on earth will be bound in heaven, and whatever you loose on earth will be loosed in heaven" (Matthew 18:18).

Eternal Life
"I tell you the truth, he who believes has everlasting life" (John 6:47).

Fear Not
"Do not be afraid of those who kill the body but cannot kill the soul. Rather, be afraid of the One who can destroy both soul and body in hell" (Matthew 10:28).

Financial Needs
"Give, and it will be given to you. A good measure, pressed down, shaken together and running over, will be poured into your lap. For with the measure you use, it will be measured to you" (Luke 6:38).

Forgiveness
"Then Jesus said to her, 'Your sins are forgiven'" (Luke 7:48).

Freedom
"Then you will know the truth, and the truth will set you free. . . . So if the Son sets you free, you will be free indeed" (John 8:32,36).

Fruitfulness
"I am the vine; you are the branches. If a man remains in me and I in

him, he will bear much fruit; apart from me you can do nothing. . . . You did not choose me, but I chose you and appointed you to go and bear fruit—fruit that will last. Then the Father will give you whatever you ask in my name" (John 15:5,16).

Fulfillment
"If anyone is thirsty, let him come to me and drink. Whoever believes in me, as the Scripture has said, streams of living water will flow from within him" (John 7:37-38).

God's Presence
"And surely I am with you always, to the very end of the age" (Matthew 28:20).

Hearing God's Voice
"When he has brought out all his own, he goes on ahead of them, and his sheep follow him because they know his voice" (John 10:4).

Heaven
"Jesus answered, 'I am the way and the truth and the life. No one comes to the Father except through me'" (John 14:6).

Holy Spirit
"If you then, though you are evil, know how to give good gifts to your children, how much more will your Father in heaven give the Holy Spirit to those who ask him" (Luke 11:13).

Joy
"I have told you this so that my joy may be in you and that your joy may be complete" (John 15:11).

Kingdom
"From the days of John the Baptist until now, the kingdom of heaven has been forcefully advancing, and forceful men lay hold of it" (Matthew 11:12).

Miracles
"I tell you the truth, anyone who has faith in me will do what I have been doing. He will do even greater things than these, because I am going to the Father" (John 14:12).

Peace

"Peace I leave with you; my peace I give you. I do not give to you as the world gives. Do not let your hearts be troubled and do not be afraid" (John 14:27).

Perseverance

"Blessed is the man who does not fall away on account of me" (Luke 7:23).

Power

"I am going to send you what my Father has promised; but stay in the city until you have been clothed with power from on high" (Luke 24:49).

Prayer

"So I say to you: Ask and it will be given to you; seek and you will find; knock and the door will be opened to you. For everyone who asks receives; he who seeks finds; and to him who knocks, the door will be opened" (Luke 11:9-10).

Rest

"Come to me, all you who are weary and burdened, and I will give you rest. Take my yoke upon you and learn from me, for I am gentle and humble in heart, and you will find rest for your souls. For my yoke is easy and my burden is light" (Matthew 11:28-30).

Security

"I give them eternal life, and they shall never perish; no one can snatch them out of my hand. My Father, who has given them to me, is greater than all; no one can snatch them out of my Father's hand" (John 10:28-29).

Unity

"I in them and you in me. May they be brought to complete unity to let the world know that you sent me and have loved them even as you have loved me" (John 17:23).

"The Bible wasn't given for our information, but for our transformation."

—D.L. Moody

♥ 13. Which of the promises of God previously listed would be most helpful for you to learn to pray right now? Why?

♥ 14. Which of the promises of God previously listed has been helpful for you to claim in the past? Explain the situation.

🗩 15. Why do you think God makes so many promises?

🗩 16. Why do you think God intends for His promises to play a significant role in your prayer life?

�֎ 17. Specifically, what role do the promises of God play in enabling you to flee the temptations of the evil one?

♥ 18. What truth is God teaching you in this lesson? Write it down.

"Let him who cannot be alone beware of community . . . let him who is not in community beware of being alone . . . each by itself has profound pitfalls and perils. One who wants fellowship without solitude plunges into the void of words and feelings and one who seeks solitude without fellowship perishes in the abyss of vanity, self-infatuation and despair."

—Dietrich Bonhoffer, *Life Together*
(Harper and Row, 1952), pp. 77-78.

♥ 19. What are you going to do with this truth?

Assignment for This Week (for individual or group study)

- Read through John 1-7. Using a red pen or pencil, mark every promise you find and write a single word in the margin to indicate the nature of the promise.
- Continue to record your insights as you use the Lord's Prayer pattern.
- Continue to record your insights as you quote John 15:1-8, reflecting upon the meaning of each word.

Group Prayer Assignment

- As a group, discuss this question: "Since God can tempt no one (James 1:13), why did Jesus teach us to pray, 'Lead us not into temptation, but deliver us from the evil one'?"
- As a group, share your answers to Question 14.
- As a group, enjoy an extended, unstructured prayer time. Encourage everyone in the group to pray simple, short prayers aloud, one after another.

Enjoying the Master's Prayer Life

Receiving the Spirit

John 14:15-31, 16:5-16

> "God does nothing but in answer to prayer."
> —John Wesley, E.M. Bounds, *Power through Prayer*
> (Moody Press, N.D.), p. 38.

CONGRATULATIONS! YOU HAVE COMPLETED 75 PERCENT OF THIS STUDY.

- You have sat at your Lord's feet, studying His prayer life from the gospels.
- You are learning to use the Lord's Prayer pattern, and you have gained many insights along the way.
- You have memorized John 15:1-8 and have gained life-giving insights from it as well.
- You are on your way to developing a meaningful prayer life!

During these final weeks, you will move beyond simply praying *like* Jesus. You will learn to make Christ's prayer life *your* prayer life. You will begin to allow Christ to pray through you. In order for this to take place, however, you need to allow His Holy Spirit to fill you.

"Let us give ourselves anew to prayer, that the church may be restored to her Pentecostal state. Let us by faith yield ourselves wholly to the Spirit and receive Him by faith to fill us. Let us give ourselves to prayer for the power of the Spirit in the life and work of the church at home and abroad. The Pentecostal command to preach the gospel to every creature is urgent, all the more from having been neglected so long. Prayer brought Pentecost; prayer still brings it. But few feel how weak our power in prayer is."

—Andrew Murray, *Key to the Missionary Problem*
(1901, reprinted Christian Literature Crusade 1979).

Read John 14:15-31.

During the final week of Jesus' life, He taught virtually nonstop on the person and work of the Holy Spirit. Jesus wanted His disciples to understand that when He went back to heaven, His ministry on earth would not be finished. On the contrary, His ministry would continue in and through the lives of the disciples—stronger than ever because of the work of the Holy Spirit.

It is essential to our study that we realize that the Holy Spirit is a person. This understanding is often lost because He is referred to throughout the Bible as fire, wind, water, a dove, breath, and other inanimate or impersonal word pictures. The fact is, however, that the Holy Spirit is just as much a person as the Father and the Son.

✍ 1. What evidence do you see in this passage that the Holy Spirit is a person?

✍ 2. What indication do you find that the Holy Spirit is God?

✍ 3. What indication do you find that the Holy Spirit is indwelling?

✍ 4. What indication do you find that the Holy Spirit is invisible?

❋ 5. What indication do you find regarding the intended role of the Holy Spirit in our lives?

❋ 6. What indication do you find that the Holy Spirit is sent to make us like Jesus?

🗨 7. Since the Holy Spirit is God, is there any reason why we can't talk with or pray to the Holy Spirit?

♥ 8. In what ways have you experienced the person and work of the Holy Spirit in your life? Explain.

> "Prayer is the method that God Himself has appointed for our obtaining the Holy Spirit."
>
> —R. A. Torrey, *How to Pray* (Whitaker House, 1983), p. 15.

Read John 16:5-16.

In this passage, Jesus continues to explain the strategic role of the Holy Spirit in the believers' lives.

✍ 9. What additional information do you learn about the Holy Spirit in this passage?

✍ 10. According to these verses, what is the role of the Holy Spirit?

♥ 11. Have you ever experienced the work of the Holy Spirit in your life in these ways? Explain.

💬 12. If the Holy Spirit worked in your local church the way Jesus described in these verses, what differences might you observe?

> "Lord, make my life a prayer meeting."
>
> —Armin Gesswein

Read John 20:19-23.

These verses describe a high-water mark in the disciples' experience with their Lord. It is here that He explicitly commands them to be filled with the Holy Spirit. He is no longer talking to them about the person of the Holy Spirit; He is giving them the Holy Spirit.

We will be taking a more in-depth look at the person and work of the Holy Spirit in our next lesson. In this lesson, we will consider just a few questions from these verses.

✍ 13. What evidence is there in these verses that the disciples were feeling less than prepared for what they were facing?

✳ 14. Jesus gives the disciples a couple of gifts. What were they?

🗩 15. Why do you think Jesus breathed on them?

✳ 16. Why was it essential that the disciples overtly receive the Holy Spirit?

🗩 17. What would have been involved in them receiving the Holy Spirit?

♥ 18. Have you ever overtly received the Holy Spirit? Explain.

♥ 19. What truth is God teaching you in this lesson? Write it down.

♥ 20. What are you going to do with this truth?

"The popular notion that the first obligation of the church is to spread the Gospel to the uttermost parts of the world is false. Our first obligation is to be spiritually worthy to spread it. Our Lord said, 'Go ye' but He also said, 'Tarry ye' and the tarrying had to come before the going. Had the disciples gone forth as missionaries before the Day of Pentecost, it would have been an overwhelming spiritual disaster, for they would have done no more than made converts after their own likeness and this would have altered for the worse the whole history of the western world and had consequences throughout the ages to come."

—A. W. Tozer, *Alliance Witness*, June 3, 1953, p. 2.

Assignment for This Week (for individual or group study)
- Read through John 8-14, marking all the promises of God in red and labeling them in the margin with an appropriate word or heading.
- Continue to record your insights as you use the Lord's Prayer pattern.
- Pray through the Lord's Prayer pattern for your family or for a certain family member.

Group Prayer Activity
- Share with the group what you are learning about the person and work of the Holy Spirit.
- Share with the group some helpful promises you've discovered in John's gospel.
- Pair up (men with men and women with women) and pray for each other to receive the full ministry of the Holy Spirit.

Cupping Our Hands

Luke 11:1-13; Matthew 6:9-12

> "The condition of the church may be very accurately gauged by its prayer meetings. So is the prayer meeting a grace-ometer and from it we may judge of the amount of divine working among a people. If God be near a church, it must be pray[ing], and if He be not there, one of the first tokens of His absence will be a slothfulness in prayer."
>
> —Charles Haden Spurgeon, Tom Carter, *Spurgeon at His Best* (Baker, 1988), p. 145.

HAVING SPENT THREE YEARS TEACHING HIS DISCIPLES TO PRAY, JESUS DID not want their prayer lives to falter at the end of His earthly ministry. He wanted to teach them more than how to pray. He wanted to teach them to *receive*; that is, to pray *with cupped hands,* as if receiving a gift.

The disciples' natural tendency would have been to leave Jerusalem, where their lives were in jeopardy, and return to their homes in Galilee. However, much to their amazement, Jesus gave His disciples a command (the original language connotes a strict military order): "Do not leave Jerusalem, but wait for the gift my Father promised" (Acts 1:4). The disciples obeyed Jesus' command; they did an about-face and went back to Jerusalem. Gathered in the Upper Room, they joined in a corporate prayer meeting that would shake the ends of the earth. The book of Acts says that they "all joined together constantly in prayer" (Acts 1:14).

This Upper Room prayer meeting was the launching pad for the early church. It was from that prayer meeting that Jesus fulfilled Acts 1:8 and sent the good news out from Jerusalem to Judea and Samaria and the ends of the earth.

Read Acts 1:1-14.

✍ 1. What command does Jesus give His disciples in v. 4?

❋ 2. Why was this command essential to the fulfillment of Jesus' mission?

✍ 3. What evidence do we have that the disciples obeyed this command from the Lord?

✍ 4. According to v. 8, what was the critical element in order for the mission of the church to be fulfilled?

❋ 5. What is demonstrated here about the relationship between prayer and the ministry of the Holy Spirit?

❋ 6. What gift were the early disciples waiting to receive with cupped hands?

Read Luke 11:1-13.

The disciples asked Jesus to teach them to pray. Before He was done answering their question, He was teaching them to pray with cupped hands. We could call this "the doctrine of receiving." Receiving goes beyond praying. Many people pray and pray and yet never receive. Sometimes it's helpful to think about prayer in terms of receiving.

- Rather than praying, you can be receiving!
- Rather than having a prayer time, you can have a receiving time!
- Rather than attending prayer meetings, you can attend receiving meetings.
- Rather than asking, "Lord, teach me to pray," you can begin asking, "Lord, teach me to receive."

It is remarkable how often in Luke's gospel *prayer* and the *Holy Spirit* appear side by side in the same verse. As noted earlier, by the time Jesus was finished answering the disciples' request to teach them to pray, He was teaching them to receive the Holy Spirit. Clearly, receiving the Holy Spirit is the key to learning to pray effectively.

✍ 7. According to vs. 9-10, what are the three kinds of prayer?

✳ 8. In what way does each of these kinds of prayer involve receiving?

🗩 9. In your own words, what is the difference between praying and receiving?

♥ 10. Do you ever find yourself praying without receiving? Why?

✳ 11. Why did Jesus teach His disciples about receiving the Holy Spirit when they asked Him to teach them to pray?

♥ 12. In what ways has the Holy Spirit been teaching you to pray?

Read Matthew 6:9-12.
It has been said that every portion of the Lord's Prayer pattern involves receiving. In this sense we are always praying with cupped hands, as if receiving a gift.

"Our Father in heaven": He becomes our Father not through any effort of our own, but because we received His fatherhood by faith.

"Hallowed be your name": We must receive revelation in order to internalize the worth of His name.

"Your kingdom come": We receive His kingdom.

"Your will be done": We receive His will.

"Give us": We receive God's provision for physical needs.

"Forgive us": We receive God's provision for spiritual needs.

"As we also have forgiven": We give to others (grace, mercy, forgiveness) what we first received from Christ.

"Lead us not": We receive His leadership.

"But deliver us": We receive His deliverance.

✎ 13. Which portion of the Lord's Prayer pattern *explicitly* refers to receiving?

14. Which portion of the Lord's Prayer pattern *implicitly* refers to receiving?

15. Why might it be helpful to physically cup your hands while praying?

♥ 16. What truth is God teaching you in this lesson? Write it down.

♥ 17. What are you going to do with this truth?

Assignment for This Week (for individual or group study)
- Read through John 15-21, marking all the promises of God in red and labeling them in the margin with an appropriate word or heading.
- Pray through the Lord's Prayer pattern for your church family.

Group Prayer Activity
- Share with the group what you have learned about the person and work of the Holy Spirit this past week.
- Share with the group some other helpful, life-giving promises you've discovered in John's gospel this past week.
- Take some time (approximately 10 minutes) to thank God for specific insights you've learned over the past month while using the Lord's Prayer pattern.

Enjoying the Upper Room

John 15:1-8

> "The greatest need in the church today is for those who know the Lord Jesus Christ to be filled with the Holy Spirit. If we are not filled with the Holy Spirit, we are sinning against God."
>
> —Billy Graham

WHEN JESUS ASCENDED INTO HEAVEN, THE ONLY THING HE LEFT behind was a prayer meeting. From the moment Jesus called the disciples to leave their fishing boats and tax offices, He strategically and deliberately mentored them in prayer. Quoting Isaiah 56:7, Jesus threw down the gauntlet at the temple when He announced, "My house will be called a house of prayer" (Matthew 21:13).

Throughout His earthly ministry, Jesus was preparing His disciples to enter the Upper Room and enjoy extended time in the corporate prayer meeting. From that prayer meeting, He launched His mission to reach a lost world through His revived church. The disciples were devoted to prayer before Pentecost (Acts 1:14), and they were devoted to prayer after Pentecost (Acts 2:42).

If our corporate prayer life exceeds our private prayer life, we are in danger of becoming self-righteous like the Pharisees. This was the reason Jesus condemned them: They loved to pray publicly, but they had no private prayer life. On the other hand, prayer was never intended to be a strictly private experience. Jesus redeemed us to set us free from selfishness and isolation. He brought us into community so that we could experience the dynamic reality of Christ's presence in our midst.

Read Acts 2:1-4.

Without question, the greatest gifts we receive from God are the gifts of eternal life and the Holy Spirit's infilling. Some theological traditions say these gifts are received simultaneously, and others say they are received separately. Regardless of your tradition, it is essential that you are convinced by experience that you have received both gifts.

You have been learning that a Spirit-filled life is a prayer-filled life. Without pre-Pentecost prayer, there would have been no post-Pentecost power. Jesus builds His prayer life into each of us by giving us His Holy Spirit—and He gives us the Holy Spirit by prayer.

Prayer and the Holy Spirit are inseparable. When that is the case, prayer can no longer be just something we *do*; it becomes a way of life. Prayer is the delightful overflow of our love relationship with Jesus Christ.

✍ 1. In v. 1, how are the early believers described?

❃ 2. What evidence is there that these early believers were praying with cupped hands?

🗨 3. What relationship do you see between prayer and the Holy Spirit in this account?

❃ 4. What evidence is given that the Holy Spirit was actually received?

♥ 5. What evidence is there in your life that you have received the Holy Spirit?

Read Acts 2:17-18.
Peter did not want the experience of Pentecost to be dismissed as a one-time, never-to-be-repeated historical event. So he used Scripture, quoting Joel 2:28-32 to explain the Pentecost phenomenon. His intention was to declare that God would *begin* to pour out His Holy Spirit in the last days and that He would *continue* to pour out His Holy Spirit throughout the last days.

✳ 6. What is meant by "the last days"?

🗩 7. Is it fair to say that we are still in the last days, or is there indication that the last days have come to an end? Is it fair to say that God is still pouring out His Holy Spirit on all people?

✐ 8. What does the passage say will be the evidence that God is pouring out His Holy Spirit? List at least six things.

🗩 9. What evidence do you see in your local church that God is pouring out His Holy Spirit in these days?

♥ 10. What evidence do you see in your own life?

♥ 11. How is God's Holy Spirit affecting your prayer life?

"O God, send us the Holy Spirit! Give us both the breath of spiritual life and the fire of unconquerable zeal. You are our God. Answer us by fire, we pray to You! Answer both by wind and fire and then we will see You to be God indeed. The kingdom comes not and the work is flagging. O, that You would send the wind and the fire! And you will do this when we are all of one accord, all believing, all expecting, all prepared by prayer."

—Charles Hadden Spurgeon, David Bryant,
The Hope at Hand (Baker Books, 1995), p. 61.

Read John 15:1-8.
This is an opportunity to review what you have learned from the words you've memorized.

♥ 12. What does it mean to you to remain in Christ?

♥ 13. What does it mean to you for His Word to remain in you?

♥ 14. What does it mean to you that Jesus said, "ask whatever you wish, and it will be given you"?

♥ 15. In what ways are you bearing much fruit, showing yourself to be His disciple?

♥ 16. Do you know for certain that if you were to die you would go to heaven? Or is that something you are still working on?

♥ 17. Do you know for certain that you are filled with the Holy Spirit?

If you are not certain you have been filled with the Holy Spirit, may I suggest some resources for additional study:

How to Be Filled With the Holy Spirit, by A. W. Tozer (Christian Publications)
Holy Spirit, Fill Me, by Fred Hartley (Christian Publications)

I invite you to pray a prayer similar to the one I prayed more than 25 years ago during a time of deep spiritual hunger:

"Jesus, I am grateful to You for my salvation, because your death and resurrection purchased a place for me in heaven. I was unworthy of Your grace but you gave it freely to me. I know I have eternal life, and I now have a deep longing in my soul to know for certain that I have been filled with the Holy Spirit. I know You have given me this promise. Cleanse me of all my sin by the blood of the Lord Jesus Christ. I turn over my entire life to You. And right now, fill me, saturate me—every area of my life, every cell of my body, every thought. Immerse me in the Holy Spirit. I receive this by faith and I will never again doubt whether or not I have been filled. Yes, I know I am filled. Praise Jesus. Hallelujah!" *(Holy Spirit, Fill Me)*

I have never been the same!

♥ 18. How has this study helped your prayer life become more authentic?

♥ 19. In what ways is Jesus giving you joy in His house of prayer?

♥ 20. Complete this sentence: "The highlight of this study for me was
_____."

♥ 21 What truth is God teaching you in this lesson? Write it down.

♥ 22. What are you going to do with this truth?

Assignment for This Week (for individual or group study)
- Regularly use the Lord's Prayer pattern—for the rest of your life!
- Continue to pray, "Lord, teach us to pray."
- Smile! You've finished this study. No more assignments!

Group Prayer Activity
- Share with the group some of your answers to the Study Overview questions.
- As a group, quote John 15:1-8 in unison.
- Take 30 minutes or more to pray through the Lord's Prayer pattern as a group.

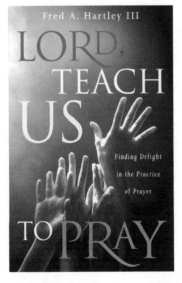

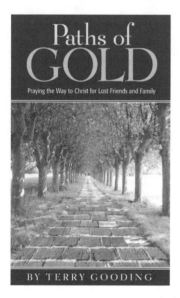

Here's a resource to help you pray with more

Power, Passion, & Purpose

Every issue of *Pray!* will provide outstanding content:

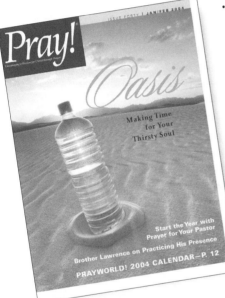

- Powerful teaching by seasoned intercessors and prayer leaders
- Encouragement to help you grow in your prayer life—no matter at what level you are currently
- Exciting news stories on the prayer movement and prayer events around the world
- Profiles on people, organizations, and churches with unique prayer ministries
- Practical ideas to help you become a more effective prayer
- Inspirational columns to stimulate you to more passionate worship of Christ
- Classic writings by powerful intercessors of the past
- And much, much more!

No Christian who wants to connect with God should be without *Pray!*

Six issues of *Pray!* are only $19.97*

(Canadian and international subscriptions are $25.97.)
*plus sales tax where applicable

Call **1-800-691-PRAY** (or 1-515-242-0297)
and mention code H5PRBKLTM when you place your order.

For information on other prayer tools, Bible studies, and prayer guides
call for a free prayer resource catalog: 719-531-3585.